Blue Goo

Tasha Pym

Illustrated by Sarah Horne

RIGBY

I am going to make Blue Goo.

First, I need a frilly frottle's feather,

some slippery slubber shoots,

one jug of jiggle jelly,

and a dollop of durble dribble.

Simmer and stir.

Sniff and sample.

Now add one glass of gunky glue.

Cover and cook.

At dinner time, dish up.

Oh no!

It's not blue!

It's not even goo!

I will call it Green Gloop!

~~Blue Goo.~~

Green Gloop.

What you need:

- A Frilly Frottle's Feather.
- Some Slippery slubber shoots
- A jug of Jiggle Jelly.
- A dollop of durble dribble.
- One glass of gunky glue..

What you do:

1. Simmer and stir
2. Sniff and sample
3. Cover and cook
4. DISH up...